GROW YOUR OWN INGREDIENTS
JAM & JELLY

A Step-by-Step Kids Gardening and Cookbook

CASSIE LIVERSIDGE

Sky Pony Press
New York

I would like to dedicate this book to Finty, Hebe, and Ottilie, who enjoyed eating my jam and jelly!

Sky Pony Press books may be purchased in bulk at special discounts for sales promotion, corporate gifts, fund-raising, or educational purposes. Special editions can also be created to specifications. For details, contact the Special Sales Department, Sky Pony Press, 307 West 36th Street, 11th Floor, New York, NY 10018 or info@skyhorsepublishing.com. Sky Pony® is a registered trademark of Skyhorse Publishing, Inc.®, a Delaware corporation. Visit our website at www.skyponypress.com.

10 9 8 6 5 4 3 2 1

Manufactured in China, February 2019

This product conforms to CPSIA 2008Library of Congress Cataloging-in-Publication Data is available on file. Cover design by Qualcom Designs

Cover illustrations by Cassie Liversidge

Print ISBN: 978-1-5107-4257-4
Ebook ISBN: 978-1-5107-4241-3

FSC
www.fsc.org
MIX
Paper from
responsible sources
FSC® C129961

CONTENTS

Welcome! This is my third book for helping you to grow your own ingredients. In this book, you will learn how to grow strawberries, pumpkins, mint, and rhubarb, and then learn how to transform them into delicious jam and jelly.

TOP TIPS FOR GROWING SUCCESS!

Always buy good-quality seed, plants, and compost to ensure success. The planting and harvest times, given in the table below, are a general guide, as they will depend on the variety of plant you are growing. When best to grow:

When to plant/sow	⬜
When to harvest	⬛

	Jan	Feb	March	April	May	June	July	Aug	Sept	Oct	Nov	Dec
Strawberry (small plants, not seeds)			Plant	Plant	Plant	Harvest	Harvest	Plant	Plant			
Pumpkin seeds				Plant	Plant	Plant			Harvest	Harvest	Harvest	Harvest
Mint (seeds and cuttings)		Plant	Plant	Plant	Plant	Harvest	Harvest	Harvest	Harvest	Harvest		
Rhubarb crown/root		Plant	Plant	Harvest	Harvest			Plant	Plant	Plant	Plant	

Strawberries

It is ideal to buy small strawberry starts or plug plants in late August and September so you can grow them before harvesting the following summer. You can also plant them during the other warmer months. Check the label on your strawberry plant to see if it will need any protection from frosts during the winter.

Rhubarb

Buy a good-quality rhubarb root or crown in fall. It won't look like much, but be patient, it will grow! You can "force" rhubarb to grow earlier and to be more tender by covering it over with a large pot or bucket. It can be planted straight into a garden if you have space. Rhubarb will die back in fall and the leaves will disappear, but it will come back the following year.

Pumpkins

Sow your pumpkins in spring or early summer, as instructed on your seed packet. The plants love to be fed with lots of manure to help them grow big! There are many different varieties but the traditional Halloween type is perfect for this recipe.

Mint

You can sow mint seeds or take cuttings when the weather is warming up in spring. The warmer summer months and longer periods of daylight make the plants grow much quicker and stronger. Mint will die back in the winter months and grow back the following year.

TOP TIPS FOR JAM AND JELLY SUCCESS!

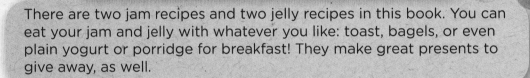

There are two jam recipes and two jelly recipes in this book. You can eat your jam and jelly with whatever you like: toast, bagels, or even plain yogurt or porridge for breakfast! They make great presents to give away, as well.

Safety:

Cooking jam and jelly requires you to heat your jams to a high temperature, so an adult must take over the recipe at this point. You can make your own colorful and imaginative labels while they are doing this.

Setting Point:

For the jam or jelly to set so that you can spread it onto bread, etc., it needs to reach a temperature of 220°F (105°C). If you use a thermometer that clips onto the side of the pan while the jam is cooking, you can watch the temperature rising and also know when to remove the jam from the heat once it has reached its setting point to prevent it from burning. If you don't have a thermometer, you can place a plate in the fridge so it becomes cold. Then, when you think the jam is getting thick enough, put a drop of it onto the cold saucer and place it back in the fridge for a couple of minutes. Then remove it and push your finger into the jam, and if the jam really wrinkles, it has reached setting point and can be put into the jars.

The apples and lemons in the recipes contain natural pectin, which also helps the jam or jelly to set. You do not need to worry about the pumpkin jam setting because it is so thick anyway.

How to Sterilize Your Jars

This should be done by an adult.

Turn your oven on to 356°F (180°C).

Wash your jars and lids using hot, soapy water and then rinse them clean. Allow them to drain.

Place the jars onto a metal baking tray (making sure they do not touch) and put into the preheated oven for 10 minutes.

Put the lids into a pan of boiling water and boil for 10 minutes.

Remove the jars from the oven, and they are then ready to be filled. Do not touch them without using an oven glove as they will be very hot.

Remove the lids from the boiling water and leave them to drain and dry before sealing up the jam or jelly.

When the jars are cool, you can label the jars with the name of the jam and the date that you made them. If the jars are sterilized correctly, the jam/jelly should last at least 3 to 4 weeks in the refrigerator.

You can use recycled jars but make sure the lids still fit correctly, old labels are removed, and rubber seals are replaced with new ones if they are the kind of jars that have them. Follow the sterilizing instructions above.

GROW YOUR OWN JAM STRAWBERRIES

You will need . . .

Potting compost

Three strawberry plants

Watering can

Straw, two handfuls

A big pot with drainage holes in the bottom

Top tip: In fall, try to buy the largest plants you can find to give them lots of time to grow and make fruit before the following summer.

STEP 1

Fill the pot with compost and plant the strawberries inside, removing their pots.

Put straw around the base of the plants to keep the soil warm and moist and to help keep the snails away! Add more mulch in the spring.

Pot your strawberries in a sunny and sheltered position outside, and water to keep the soil moist.

Top tip: Feed your strawberries with organic plant food in the spring.

STEP 2

In the spring, small white flowers grow. They attract bees and insects to pollinate them. The bees accidentally transfer pollen from the male part of the flower to the female part of the flower, which is then able to make seeds. Then, watch carefully as the yellow flower center turns into the fruit!

When the small yellow fruits have turned into large red fruits, they are ready to harvest and turn into jam.

Joke: What do you call strawberries playing guitars? *A jam session.*

MAKE YOUR OWN
STRAWBERRY JAM

To make three jars of strawberry jam, you will need:

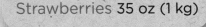
Strawberries 35 oz (1 kg)

Gelling Sugar (Jam Sugar) 25 oz (700 g)

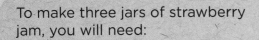

Long spoon

A big pan

1 Fresh Lemon

Lemon squeezer

Scales to weigh your ingredients

3 sterilized jam jars
(10 fl oz/325 ml)

Funnel

Cutting board & knife

A jam thermometer

Wash your hands and put on an apron.

Weigh out your ingredients.

Wash your strawberries.

Remove the tops of the strawberries, taking care not to waste any delicious fruit.

Chop the strawberries up into little pieces and place in the pan.

Cut the lemon in half and squeeze out its juice. Add to the pan.

Add the sugar to the pan.

Stir the mixture. Ask an adult to take over the cooking. They will put the pan on the burner or cooktop and turn on the heat to full power. Set a timer to 15 minutes. You can draw some labels for the jars.

9

The mixture will grow at least twice as big in the pan. Allow the jam to boil at 220°F (105°C) so that it makes lots of bubbles and thickens.

10

After 15 minutes, remove from the heat. If there is any scum (white froth), scoop from the edge using a metal spoon (as this spoils the look of the jam). Pour or ladle into sterilized jars using a funnel.

11

Seal up the jars and label them. Allow to cool before storing in a refrigerator. Eat within 2 to 3 weeks.

12

Enjoy your jam on toast, bagels, scones, or even on ice cream!

GROW YOUR OWN JAM PUMPKIN

You will need . . .

Pumpkin seeds

Trowel

Small pots

Watering can

Manure

Potting Compost

Space in a garden. If you don't have a garden, plant into as big a pot as you have!

Top tip: To grow strong pumpkin plants, it is best to start growing pumpkin seeds inside in the early summer. Follow the instructions on the seed packet as to the when your variety should be planted. You can plant straight into the garden if you prefer.

Fill your pots with compost, and then make a hole with your finger and plant one seed in each hole, covering them over with compost.

Water well and keep the soil moist at all times. Place on a sunny windowsill.

STEP 2

When your pumpkin seedlings are larger and the weather is warmer, you can plant them outside in a sunny spot.

Dig a big hole for your pumpkin, put some manure in the bottom of the hole, and then plant your seedling in. Fill the hole around with more manure; this will help feed your hungry pumpkin! Water it regularly and add more manure after a month.

STEP 3

Your pumpkin leaves will creep around your garden, and they can even climb up walls! Lovely yellow flowers will grow, and these can be male or female. Bees will come and visit the male flowers, collect pollen, and then transfer them to the female flower, which will then be able to grow into pumpkins!!

Female flower

Male flower

Keep watering them and giving them manure and by late summer or early fall, you should have lots of large pumpkins.

STEP 4

The pumpkins need to ripen, but when they sound hollow when you tap them, then they can be harvested. Cut the stems off and store them somewhere warm, dry, and sunny until you are ready to make them into jam.

Top tip: The pumpkin can be stored and used at Halloween to make into a Jack-o-lantern. You can use the delicious inside to make into pumpkin jam so that it is not wasted.

Joke: What is a pumpkin's favorite sport?
Squash!

MAKE YOUR OWN PUMPKIN JAM

To make three jars (10 fl oz size) of pumpkin jam, you will need:

Measuring jug

Water 4.2 fl oz (125 ml)

2 Lemons

Pumpkin 3.5 lb (1.5 kg)

Sugar 1 lb (453 g)

Cinnamon (ground) 1 tsp.

Thermometer

Lemon zester

A big pan with a lid

Potato masher

Lemon squeezer

Funnel

Long spoon

Metal spoon

Cutting board & knife

Ladle

3 sterilized jam jars

Scales to weigh your ingredients

Wash your hands and put on an apron. Make sure you have sterilized your jars (see page 7) so they are ready.

Weigh out your sugar and measure out the water. Wash your pumpkin and lemons.

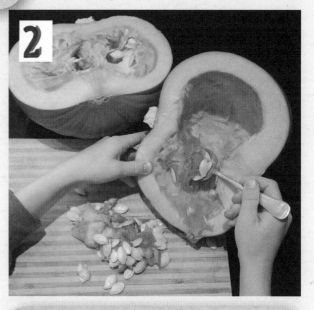

Ask an adult to halve the pumpkin. Remove the seeds inside using a metal spoon.

Ask an adult to carefully remove the skin and stalk of the pumpkin. Weigh out 3.5 lb of pumpkin.

Chop the pumpkin into little pieces and put into the pan. You can use the insides of a Halloween pumpkin. Scrape out and weigh to get 3.5 lb, then follow the recipe from this point.

Remove the zest of both lemons and add to the pumpkin in the pan.

Cut the lemons in half and squeeze out the juice. Add to the pan.

Add the water to the pumpkin and put the pumpkin on the burner/cooktop on medium heat with the lid on. Stir every so often.

After 15 to 20 minutes, add the sugar and the cinnamon to the pumpkin and stir well. Put it back on the burner on a low heat with the lid on. Stir it every 15 minutes, as it can stick to the bottom of the pan.

9

After about 1 hour, the pumpkin should be really soft. Remove from the heat and mash with a potato masher until smooth. Return to the heat for another 30 minutes, adding some water if it is too thick or starts sticking.

10

When it looks thick and smooth, remove from the heat and pour or ladle into sterilized jars using a funnel. Label them and allow them to cool before storing in a refrigerator. Eat within 2 to 3 weeks.

11

Enjoy your jam on toast, muffins, and bagels. It's delicious on plain yogurt for breakfast or dessert, too!

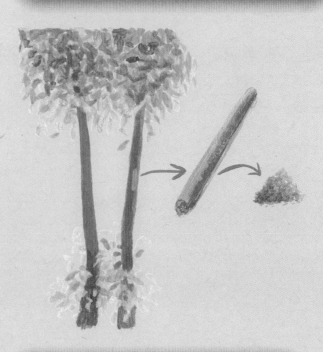

Did you know that cinnamon comes from the inner bark of the Cinnamomum tree?

GROW YOUR OWN JELLY MINT

You will need . . .

Three mint cuttings—this is the quickest way to grow a new mint plant. (If a friend has a mint plant you can ask them for the cuttings.)

Potting Compost

A pot with drainage holes in the bottom

Watering can

MINT SEED

Top tip: It takes longer, but you can also grow mint from seed. Follow the instructions on the seed packet.

STEP 1

Remove the lower leaves of the cutting to leave around six on the stem at the top. Fill the pot with compost and plant the cuttings, firming down the compost so the cutting stands upright. Water the pot of mint.

Put your pot of mint on a windowsill and water to keep the soil moist.

Top tip: Mint plants can take over a garden, so keep them in a pot. Transplant to a bigger pot when they need more space.

STEP 2

When your plant has grown larger and bushier,
it is ready to harvest to make into jelly.

Harvest your mint by nipping out the top of stems.
The rest of the plant will carry on growing happily.

Joke: What did the plate say to the other plate?
Dinner's on me tonight.

MAKE YOUR OWN
MINT JELLY

To make two or three small jars of mint jelly, you will need:

Mint—A bunch of fresh leaves (approx. 3 oz)

1 Lemon

Vinegar—White malt 3.4 fl oz (100 ml)

3 Cooking apples (Granny Smith or similar variety) approx. 27 oz (770 g)

Thermometer

Sugar 13 oz (375 g)

Water 17 fl oz (500 ml)

Lemon squeezer

Measuring jug

Jelly bag/muslin/cheesecloth

Cutting board & knife

Long spoon

Sieve

Funnel

2 or 3 small sterilized jam jars (4 fl oz, 0.125 L)

A large saucepan with a lid

Bowl with a spout

Scale to weigh your ingredients

1

Wash your hands and put on an apron. Make sure you have sterilized your jars (see page 7) so they are ready for later.

Weigh out the sugar on a scale and measure out the vinegar into the measuring jug.

2

Wash your mint leaves. Take out three stems of mint and put aside for later.

3

Tear off the mint leaves from the stems and place them in a saucepan.

4

Wash the apples and then chop up into pieces, including seeds, etc. Place them into the pan with the mint leaves.

Squeeze the juice from the lemon and add to the pan. Then chop up the rest of the whole lemon and add it to the pan, seeds as well!

Add the vinegar and the water.

Then ask an adult to put the pan on the burner/stove with the lid on. Heat for 45 minutes until the apple is really mushy. Stir very gently once or twice. The leaves will turn brown.

Remove the mint mixture from the heat and carefully strain the mixture through a sieve and jelly bag/cheesecloth into a bowl. Allow it to drip for 30 to 40 minutes.

While it is straining, you can chop the extra mint leaves into little pieces. These will be added later. Get your jars and funnel ready.

Measure out 17 fl oz (500 ml) of mint liquid and put it into the clean pan. You can use any spare liquid in a fun drink! Find a recipe at www.cassieliversidge.com. Ask an adult to put it back on the heat and bring to the boil.

When the mixture is boiling, remove the pan from the heat, add the sugar to the mint liquid, and stir until dissolved.

Put back onto the burner/stove and bring up to a boil. Stir once or twice to ensure it doesn't burn. Use a thermometer if you have one to help see when it hits 220°F (104.5°C), as this means the setting point has been reached. (See page 6 for details on setting). It should take around 15 minutes.

Remove the pan from the heat and stir in the chopped mint.

Pour or ladle the mint jelly into sterilized jars using a funnel. Be very careful, as it is very hot.

Seal the jars. Allow to cool and then label them and store in the refrigerator. Eat within 2 to 3 weeks.

Enjoy your mint jelly with roast lamb or roast potatoes, or make it into thumbprint cookies! Thumbprint cookie recipe on www.cassieliversidge.com.

GROW YOUR OWN JELLY RHUBARB

You will need . . .

Rhubarb root or "crown"

A big pot at least 20 inches (50 cm) deep with drainage holes in the bottom, or you can grow rhubarb straight into a garden.

Nutrient-rich potting compost

Watering can

Top tip: You can only buy rhubarb crowns in fall, but this is the best time to plant them! Rhubarb needs cold temperatures to trigger it to start growing.

STEP 1

Fill the pot with compost and then plant the rhubarb root inside, so that you can just see the top of it. Firm down the soil and give it some water.

Leave your rhubarb outside for the winter, feeding it with some manure or organic fertilizer in early spring.

STEP 2

By late spring, your rhubarb should have grown big, lovely leaves with long, pink stems. Harvest by easing the stalks off at the base of the stems. Cut off the leaves. The rhubarb stems are now ready to make into rhubarb jelly!

Top tip: Rhubarb leaves are poisonous, so remove them off of the edible pink stems and put them in the compost bin. In late fall, the plant will die down, but it will come up again the following spring!

Joke: What kind of sandwiches can you make at the beach?
Peanut butter and jellyfish sandwiches.

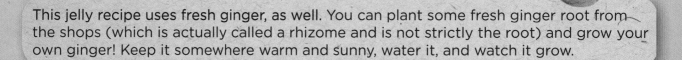

This jelly recipe uses fresh ginger, as well. You can plant some fresh ginger root from the shops (which is actually called a rhizome and is not strictly the root) and grow your own ginger! Keep it somewhere warm and sunny, water it, and watch it grow.

MAKE YOUR OWN
RHUBARB JELLY

To make three or four small (0.125 L) jars of rhubarb & ginger jelly, you will need:

Rhubarb 6–8 large stems (weighing 600 g, 21 oz) when the leaves and base are removed)

Ginger (fresh root) 1.7 oz (50 g)

Sugar 13 oz (375 g)

2 Cooking apples (Granny Smith or similar variety) 21 oz (600 g)

A big pan with a lid

Water 17 fl oz (500 ml)

Cutting board & knife

Sieve

Funnel

Thermometer

Bowl

Scales to weigh your ingredients

Long wooden spoon

Jelly bag/muslin/cheesecloth

4 small sterilized jam jars (4 fl oz, 0.125 L)

Wash your hands and put on an apron. Make sure you have sterilized your jars (see page 7) so they are ready for later.

Chop off the poisonous rhubarb leaves and remove the base of the stems. (You can compost the leaves).

Wash the rhubarb stems.

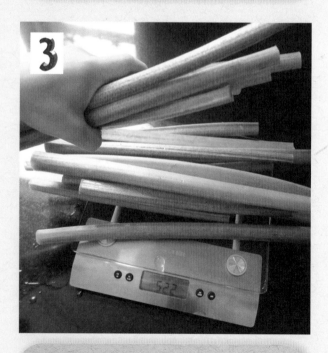

Weigh out your rhubarb so that you have around 21 oz (600 g); it is okay to be a bit over.

Weigh out the sugar and ginger.

Chop up your rhubarb into 1 inch (2 cm) long pieces, being careful to keep your fingers out of the way! Put the rhubarb in a big pan and add the water.

Chop up the ginger into small slices. It is fine to leave on the skin. Add into the pan.

Wash the apples and then chop them up and put into the pan, seeds and all!

Ask an adult to place the pan on the burner/stove to cook on a low heat. Put the lid on and only stir a couple of times.

9

Cook for around 45 minutes until the mixture is mushy.

10

Remove from the heat, strain the mixture through a jelly bag/cheesecloth (which is lining a sieve) to collect the precious juice in a bowl beneath. Allow to drain for around 40 minutes.

11

When it has stopped dripping, measure out 17 fl oz (500 ml) of liquid into a measuring jug. Pour this juice into the cleaned pan. You can use any spare juice in a beverage! Drink recipes on www.cassieliversidge.com.

12

Put back onto the burner/stove and bring up to a boil. When boiling, add the sugar and stir until it has dissolved.

Then, boil the mixture for 10 to 15 minutes. You can use a thermometer to note when it reaches 220°F (104.5°C), as this is the setting point, or test using a cold plate (see page 6 for more details).

Remove the pan from the heat, being very careful because it is very hot.

Pour or ladle the jelly into sterilized jars through a funnel. Seal up the jars. Allow to cool and then label them and store in the refrigerator. Eat within 2 to 3 weeks.

Enjoy eating your rhubarb jelly with anything. It's really delicious on porridge!!

ACKNOWLEDGMENTS

I would like to thank the following for all their help and support in the production of this book: Nicole Frail, Chris Schultz, Abigail Gehring (Skyhorse Publishing), Isabel Atherton (Creative Authors), Peter Liversidge, George and Thomas Liversidge, the Willis family, Christopher Tignor, Levin Haegele, Jill Feuerstein, Keris Salmon.

I would also like to thank the pupils at all my Grow Your Own Playground schools, who keep me inspired and determined to keep giving children the opportunity to learn about growing plants and eating homegrown food.

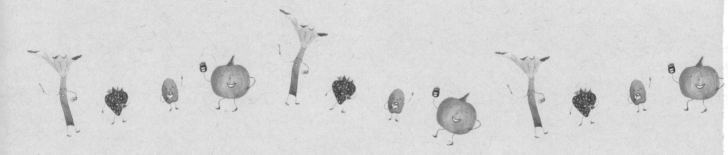